Are You an Asset or a Liability?

Are You an Asset or a Liability?

Tips for Living Life as an Outstanding Youth

Olayinka Ekenkwo

ARE YOU AN ASSET OR A LIABILITY?
TIPS FOR LIVING LIFE AS AN OUTSTANDING YOUTH

Copyright © 2016 Olayinka Ekenkwo.

All rights reserved. No part of this book may be used or reproduced by any means, graphic, electronic, or mechanical, including photocopying, recording, taping or by any information storage retrieval system without the written permission of the author except in the case of brief quotations embodied in critical articles and reviews.

iUniverse books may be ordered through booksellers or by contacting:

iUniverse
1663 Liberty Drive
Bloomington, IN 47403
www.iuniverse.com
1-800-Authors (1-800-288-4677)

Because of the dynamic nature of the Internet, any web addresses or links contained in this book may have changed since publication and may no longer be valid. The views expressed in this work are solely those of the author and do not necessarily reflect the views of the publisher, and the publisher hereby disclaims any responsibility for them.

Any people depicted in stock imagery provided by Thinkstock are models, and such images are being used for illustrative purposes only. Certain stock imagery © Thinkstock.

ISBN: 978-1-4917-9633-7 (sc)
ISBN: 978-1-4917-9634-4 (e)

Library of Congress Control Number: 2016907054

Print information available on the last page.

iUniverse rev. date: 07/13/2016

I humbly dedicate this to all the Christian teenagers and youths in all walks of life, and I extend my support and voice to say you can be all you ever dreamed to be! You belong to the topmost top!

To your success!

CONTENTS

Foreword ix

Acknowledgments xi

Introduction xiii

Chapter One   The Company You Keep 1

Chapter Two   Your Time 5

Chapter Three   The Books You Read 9

Chapter Four   The Movies You Watch 12

Chapter Five   What Do You Do with Money? 14

Chapter Six   Some Liabilities Feeders to Avoid 17
- Procrastination 17
- Indecisiveness 19
- Fear 19
- Low Self-Esteem 21
- Ignorance 22
- Examples of Liabilities 23
- Satan 23
- Samson and Delilah 24
- King Solomon and His Concubines 26

Chapter Seven   Asset Building Blocks 27
- Planning 27
- Discipline 28
- Self-Confidence 29
- Mentors and Role Models 31
- Persistence 32
- Determination 33

	Examples of Assets...35
	David and Jonathan 35
	Joshua and Caleb...36
	Jesus Christ 37
	The Holy Spirit..38
Chapter Eight	A Destiny to Fulfill..40
Chapter Nine	Confessions for Success...................................43
Chapter Ten	Daniel—A Case Study....................................45
Chapter Eleven	The Right to Choose......................................48
Chapter Twelve	Go and Succeed..50
About the Young, Free and Single Forum 53

FOREWORD

The challenges facing today's youth are enormous and are amply compounded by the advent of technology, which has in some way become the conduit for distraction. It is often said that the youth are tomorrow's leaders, but the preparation for leadership begins today, with the inculcation of Christian values, standards and ethos that will be instrumental in their service to civil society and to the body of Christ, the Church.

But for the Christian youth, it is a continuous struggle to conform to the word of God and live within His will with the constant pressure from the media and their dwindling supply of spiritual and moral capital. They are submerged in a world of convoluted messages—one that accentuates rebellion against parents and authority while extolling immorality and lewd lifestyles.

With religion failing to inspire confidence in the youth, and with adults around them neglecting their responsibilities, this book is not only timely but meticulously written to provide godly counsel to the youth on their journeys. It integrates vignettes of real-life experiences that resonate with readers, providing unique opportunities for genuine reflection.

By citing appropriate verses from the Bible, the authoritative source that holds the principles to our destiny, this book seeks to encourage, support and endear Christian youth to their faith when life's challenges seem insurmountable. The role and importance of wise sayings and proverbs are generously emphasized at every instance, which represents the theme of each chapter, providing truth, wisdom, warnings, direction and motivation to forge ahead and overcome the obstacles.

By recognizing the duality of humans as spiritual and physical beings, the book appears to mandate education, which in today's world has become the gateway to success, the pathway to disillusionment and the basis for social mobility. It strongly encourages youth to seek knowledge, acquire the capacity to contextualize notions in real-world settings and make a critical difference in their communities.

Are You an Asset or a Liability? is inspirational and thought-provoking, and it asks pertinent questions that inspire the Christian youth to find biblical truths in their journeys to fulfill their God-given destinies in becoming assets to humanity and His kingdom.

If you are a teenager or a young adult feeling susceptible to peer pressure or facing other life challenges, this is a must-read.

Dr. Phil Tam-Al Alalibo and Dr. Trudy Alalibo

ACKNOWLEDGMENTS

There are not enough words to appreciate and give honour to the multitude of people I am compelled to acknowledge. Many people have contributed in various ways to my life and to this book. I am grateful to the many women and men of God who have inspired and mentored me and whose prodding has consequently motivated me in writing *Are You an Asset or a Liability?*

I adore and worship my saviour, who gives me grace daily to exist and hope for a brighter tomorrow. I wholeheartedly acknowledge and cherish my family and friends, who encouraged me in my journey of life, and I owe a deep gratitude to them for being there for me.

I desire to express special appreciation to Rev. Dr. Johnson Adesina and his amiable wife, Rev. Mrs. Margaret Adesina, of the Foursquare Gospel Church in Nigeria, from whose ministry the idea of this book originated. To the numerous youth who graced and attended the Young, Free and Single Forum I organized while living in Lagos, Nigeria, and to all the sponsors and donors of the programs, such as Rev. Tunde and Deaconness Yemi Lemo, the late Francis and Adenike Odunuga, Charles Eke, Wole and Tola Rotimi, and all the Foursquare Gospel Church in Nigeria. Also, thanks to my current pastors, Phillip and Yemisi Aladesua, of Jesus House Scarborough, Redeemed Christian Church of God in Canada, and to my friends, among whom are Segun and Molara Mojeed, Professors Phil and Trudy Alalibo, and Zefe Osime-Fakolade, I say God bless you richly.

I thank God Almighty for my husband, James, who allows me to spread my wings as an eagle and fly as far as the Divine allows. I love my God-given children, Udochuckwu, Chioma and Ozioma, and I pray that each of you will fulfill your God-given destiny.

I give honour to those who honour and where credit is due.

Olayinka Ekenkwo

INTRODUCTION

Are you an asset or a liability? You probably are wondering after reading the title. For youth who do not like mathematics and won't talk about calculus or other subjects that deal with calculations and figures, I encourage you to continue reading and not be discouraged. It is not a mistake or by coincidence that you are holding this book in your hands. *Are You an Asset or a Liability?* has the potential to fulfill that dream of a successful life and can impact you by causing you to experience a major paradigm shift.

I have this passion for the youth that compels me to want to share what I have learnt and impact lives. I grew up without much instruction or direction in life, and therefore I learnt from my experiences mainly through trial and error. As I was growing up, I discovered that no one really cared about whether I became successful or not. I was provided the basic necessities of life, such as clothing, food, housing and education. I developed the habit of reading when I realized that I was learning a lot from the books I read. The books exposed me to a world I did not know about, and I became an avid reader. This habit has turned out to be my greatest asset. Knowledge from books tremendously shaped my thinking. As I studied some youth I had the opportunity to interact with, I came to the realization that I owe it to every youth to reveal the secrets that I learnt through books, if they care to listen. I had the strong obligation to transfer my knowledge and experience, thereby helping a youth chart a course for his or her life. I began by organizing seminars and created an avenue to not only transfer knowledge but also inspire and motivate youth to take their destinies in their own hands and run with it. I charged them during those seminars to become who they want to be. I encouraged them to not be mediocre and to dream big. It was such fun that word went round, and future sessions were usually fully packed.

It was while preparing for one of these seminars that the idea of this book hatched in my head. It has taken me almost fifteen years to get this book out to you. All through those years, I knew that this book, no matter how long it took, must be published because someone needs to get the message it brings. It was only a matter of time. The intention of this book is to stir up the giant in you and let you know that if it has to be, it is up to you! Your daydreams can become reality if you follow the advice I am about to share with you. I experienced wonderful successes as I put these ideas into practice in my own personal life. It works!

Many youth who desire to make it in life and live successful lives often fall into potholes. *Are You an Asset or a Liability?* discusses some major topics that point you in the right direction, thereby avoiding the pitfalls. The pitfalls could create hindrances to your mega dreams and become insurmountable mountains. It is true that there are challenges facing modern youth, especially with technology, entertainment and what have you, but they are not insurmountable. No youth should feel helpless in the face of these challenges, because they are only challenges and do have the potential to bring the very best out of you. Take charge and take control, and stretch yourself to the very limit. You will be amazed at what you can achieve. Dare to succeed!

Success is yours only if you choose the right path—that is, being an asset and not a liability. Most human beings, if not all, want to be valued, appreciated and respected for who they are. The degree to which you will experience being valued, appreciated and respected by people around you, as well as being accorded honour, is directly proportional to how much you embrace the truths being conveyed in this book. In essence, when you add value to people's lives, you become an asset, and everyone would like to identify with you.

Only you can attain this, by being courageous, making the move and taking bold steps to make your life count. You can be a person of impact by working on yourself now. Exert yourself now, and you will reap the benefits in the future. Do not be slack because there is no mountain you cannot climb, and it is not too late to make the changes. Do not be self-centred. Making everything about you all the time will hinder you from reaching your God-given potential. There are times when you have to be deliberately selfless and make it about others instead of you; that way, you become an asset!

> Your greatness is measured by your horizons.
> —Michelangelo

If you desire to make it big in life, now is the time to lay the foundation for it by working on yourself, focusing on developing yourself and being an asset first to yourself. You become an asset to yourself by doing a self-assessment; by changing your paradigm; by making the effort to raise your value. You need to make that shift and think big. Once you are able to raise the bar in your life, you become an asset to yourself. It is after you have worked at it for yourself and conquered, then you can begin to become an asset to the world around you. Let me say here that in order for anyone to accomplish anything worthwhile in life, it takes deliberate, conscious and well-thought-out planning and action. Things do not just happen; you *make* them happen. It is often said that to fail to prepare is to prepare to fail. You must drop the entitlement mentality. You are not entitled to everything! Your parents don't have to provide everything, the government does not owe you much and society cannot bow at your feet. Rather, you have to prove your worth! Go for it! Be an asset, not a liability!

> To be what we are, and to become what we are capable of becoming, is the only end in life.
> —Robert Louis Stevenson

This book is borne out of my passion for teenagers, especially those in the household of faith, and it is my desire to see each one of you who comes across my path succeed. I want to make available some truths that adults do not teach you at school but that are vital to your life. In *Are You an Asset or a Liability?* you will discover some basic, simple truths that, if you take them to heart and practice them, can catapult you to heights you have never dreamed to achieve. Do not drop this book until you imbibe its contents. Be open, be humble, be teachable and remain positive. I have taken time to include some quotes from notable individuals who added value to society and became assets of their generation. You cannot afford to be both mentally and physically lazy, so stir yourself up and stop waiting for someone else to do what only you can do!

> Great minds have purpose, others have wishes.
> —Washington Irving

There is the story of a man in the Bible who was described as being a cripple in the Gospel of Mark. His name was Bartimaeus. This blind man took his destiny in his own hands, and his life changed for the better. I encourage you to take the time to read what happened in Mark 10:46–52 (New International Version).

The blind man did not allow himself to be shut down by society or his circumstances. He seized the moment and exerted himself despite the opposition and challenges around him. Some teenagers ought to be like this man: they should not wait to be assisted or allow the circumstances or environment to pull you down; rather, you must take charge if you desire a successful life. Things do not just happen. No way. You have to move for yourself, or else you will be in one spot for a long time. Stop blaming your parents, teachers, neighbours, supervisors, friends, pastors and leaders in the church or the government. If it has got to be, it is up to you! I want to challenge you to get up, shake off any shackles, take that step of faith and be what you want to be! Stop waiting and wasting time. Time is running out, and the world is waiting for you. You are on this planet for a reason and a specific purpose, not to simply occupy space or be a nuisance. You are more than that!

Chapter One

THE COMPANY YOU KEEP

> Walk with the wise and become wise, for a companion of fools suffers harm.
> —Proverbs 13:20 (NIV)

In financial terms, an asset is something that gives one wealth and continues to produce wealth. In simple terms, it appreciates in value. A liability is something that takes wealth away from you and gradually depreciates in value.

Some people have great destinies and are born to make a mark in their generation. However, by reason of the company they keep—the groups and persons they hang around with—this is made impossible. Why? Many people say, "Birds of a feather flock together," and "Show me your friend, and I will tell you who you are." These sayings are further confirmed in the Bible: "Do not be misled: bad company corrupts good character" (1 Cor. 15:33 NIV).

In other words, people may have imbibed good habits and possesses a good character as a result of their upbringing by discipline and godly parents. As they begin to keep bad company, they lose the virtues they have been brought up with over time. They find themselves doing negative things they never thought they could do. They lose value—and eventually their colourful destinies.

> A ship in port is safe, but that's not what ships are built for.
> —Grace Hopper

A teenager who can be raised from a disciplined home, can then gain admission into university and suddenly become something else just because parents are not nearby. Teenagers who tend to keep company with their peers who do not consider smoking, drugs and fornication as a big deal will soon be caught in a trap that will require the grace and mercies of God in order to escape from them.

It is easier to fall when you are on top. It is easier for someone who is already down to pull another down, rather than for the one who is on top to pull up the one who is down. The people you associate with will either pull you up or down, depending on where they are standing. You should continuously assess those whom you call your friends and adjust yourself accordingly. In other words, you have a right to choose who your friends are. Friendship is not by force. As a matter of fact, you should hang around those who are better than you. It is a natural law that as you associate with people, you begin to think, reason, act and talk like them.

> If you don't design your own life plan, chances are you'll fall into someone else. And guess what they might have planned for you? Not much.
> —Jim Rohn

On the other hand, perhaps you have been brought up in a setting where there are no rules, and you are allowed to do what you want, whenever you want. This has resulted in getting you into trouble within the larger society. It is not too late to turn over a new leaf. Take one day at a time and do the right thing. Soon it will become a habit, and you will see that your attitude will change.

> As for worrying about what other people might think—forget it. They aren't concerned about you. They're too busy worrying about what you and other people think of them.
> —Michael le Boeuf

If you really want to measure yourself, look at your friends and the people with whom you surround yourself. If you keep company with those who have no respect for others, who are careless about their lives and future, who hate school and encourage you to skip school or classes, who like to gallivant instead of studying and who wallow in whiling away time and have no future ambition, then you will end up just like them. These types of people I have just described are the people I call liabilities. These people encourage you to dress carelessly, eat unhealthy food and indulge in dangerous habits that eventually lead to destruction. They do not see the big deal in immoral acts, such as fornication, adultery, drugs, gangs and alcoholism. This category of people possess mental odour. Hear this! Stay away from those who have bad mental odour. They are liabilities, and liabilities never accomplish even their smallest dreams.

> Sometimes the best helping hand you can get is a good, firm push.
> —Joann Thomas

On the other hand, you have some friends and peers who always excite you, encourage you to be your best, see the positive side of things, keep hope alive, make you feel good and point you towards your future and dreams. They encourage you to not quit even in the face of obstacles, and they give constructive criticism. I call these people assets. These are the people I like to be around all the time. What about you? Who are your pals? Think about this. Your friends should be people who tell you positive things and make you want to achieve greater heights. Your friends are not the people who introduce you to drugs, street life, night life and truancy. Your friends inspire you and point you towards success. What kind of friend are you?

Action

1. Evaluate your relationships.

2. Who are those you need to detach from?

3. What places do you need to stop going to in order to succeed in this goal?

Chapter Two

YOUR TIME

> There is a time for everything, and a season for every activity under the heavens: a time to be born and a time to die, a time to plant and a time to uproot,
> a time to kill and a time to heal,
> a time to tear down and a time to build,
> a time to weep and a time to laugh,
> a time to mourn and a time to dance,
> a time to scatter stones and a time to gather them,
> a time to embrace and a time to refrain from embracing,
> a time to search and a time to give up,
> a time to keep and a time to throw away,
> a time to tear and a time to Mend,
> a time to be silent and a time to speak,
> a time to love and a time to hate,
> a time for war and a time for peace.
> —Ecclesiastes 3:1–8 (NIV)

Time is a resource! Time is measured in seconds, minutes, hours, days, weeks, months and years. Time is life, a precious commodity. As you invest your time or waste it, you determine whether you are moving towards being an asset or a liability. I once had a discussion with a male and a female of about the same age. One was full of tales of woe; was obviously famished, frail and ill; and lacked money to get the basic things of life. The other was full of life, joy, health and hope. What made the difference? It was the proper use of time! As the Bible says, "Do not be deceived: God is not mocked. A man reaps what he sows" (Gal. 6:7 NIV).

The saying goes that you've made your bed, and so you must lie on it. How do you use your time? Are you investing it or wasting it? Remember—today is the tomorrow you talked about yesterday! Use your time wisely. You need to ask yourself, "What am I doing now? Is it leading me to becoming an asset or a liability?"

> Things that matter most should never be at the mercy of things that matter least
> —Goethe

I have taken the time to put my thoughts together and come up with this book. If I had not taken the time to do so, I may never have the opportunity to be an asset to you. Some of the things mentioned here may not be new to you, however there is no harm in reminding you about what you already know.

> Don't say you don't have enough time. You have exactly the same number of hours per day that were given to Helen Keller, Louis Pasteur, Michelangelo, Leonardo da Vinci, Thomas Jefferson and Albert Einstein.
> —Jackson Brown Jr.

If you want to succeed and be a top performer in any endeavour in life, you must create the time to develop yourself in the area of your interest. A lot of people complain about how they do not have time to invest in endeavours that will guarantee their success, but the truth is you will create the time for what you consider important. If you want that degree intensely enough, if you desire that scholarship, award or certificate, then you will create time to study and give it what it takes.

> The bad news is time flies. The good news is you're the pilot.
> —Michael Altshuler

It is said that time waits for no one. If you doubt it, sit down and look at the clock tick, and you will be convinced.

> Until we can manage time, we can manage nothing else.
> —Peter F. Drucker

If you fail to invest your time in the right direction, you will become a liability. You must value other people's time as well. People will respect you if you value their time. Know the right time to take action and the right time to stay put. Timing is so important that it determines when you seize the opportunity of a lifetime. I pray you understand this issue.

Read this.

> If you don't design your own life plan, chances are you'll fall into someone else's. And guess what they might have planned for you? Not Much.
> —Jim Rohn

Value time, and do not hang around those who do not value time. If you are asked to attend an interview, and you get there five minutes late, you have lost that opportunity even before you were interviewed. In my role in human resources management for many years, I have had the privilege of interviewing hundreds of applicants. I realized how important it is to have a good sense of time. It makes a difference. Nothing stops you from arriving early for an appointment. As a matter of fact, you look more responsible than a person who arrives late. I encourage you to strive for excellence in this area.

You will not fail.

Action

1. Evaluate how you use your time.

2. What activities do you need to eliminate or reduce?

3. What activities do you need to engage in more?

4. Commit to taking responsibility for using your time well.

Chapter Three

THE BOOKS YOU READ

> Now Daniel so distinguished himself among the administrators and the satraps by his exceptional qualities that the king planned to set him over the whole kingdom.
> —Daniel 6:3 (NIV)

Daniel was a youth when he was taken captive to Babylon. He eventually landed in the King's palace as one of the slaves. However, there was something unique about Daniel: he was a reader! Daniel spent his spare time reading books. He took time to develop his intellectual property. He must have thought that though men may take him captive physically, they were unable to capture his mind. He developed his mind to the extent that he was distinguished in the land. This brought about promotion and freedom.

> Just as iron rusts from disuse, even so does inaction spoil the intellect.
> —Leonardo da Vinci

Are you a reader? What kinds of books and materials do you enjoy reading in your leisure time? A lot of people enjoy reading magazines, books and materials that do not add any value to their lives. If you read, please do not read just anything. Be selective. There are lots of good books, magazines, journals, motivational, biographies and educative materials that will be of benefit and worth the time you invest in reading them. The library has millions of books awaiting your discovery. I challenge you to read, because you will discover that your knowledge base will expand.

> Tomorrow is the most important thing in life. It comes in to us at midnight very clean. It's perfect when it arrives and it puts itself in our hands, and hopes we've learned something from yesterday.
> —John Wayne

Some youths go on the Internet only to open sites that will kill their futures. The Internet is a wonderful invention for us all, however it can be a death trap for many people's futures if not checked. My advice is to read, read, read—but read to stay alive, read to invest positively in your life and read to be an asset, not a liability!

It is often said that readers are leaders, and leaders are readers. Take the time to study the leaders of past and present generations. You will find that they read. The thing about reading good materials is that you learn from the experiences of the authors. When you pick up any good book to read, by the time you are through, you are certainly better than when you started the book. There so many motivational, educative and inspirational books that you can easily buy or even borrow.

> Education comes from within; you get it by struggle and effort and thought.
> —Napoleon Hill

My advice to you is to invest in books in order to develop yourself! I have read several books that have affected me positively. The greatest book that I have read is the Holy Bible. The book of Joshua paints a vivid picture of the benefits of studying God's word when it says, "Keep this Book of the law always on your lips; meditate on it day and night, so that you may be careful to do everything written in it. Then you will be prosperous and successful" (Josh. 1:8 NIV).

I want to encourage you to engage yourself in reading. Readers are leaders! You will stand out!

Action

1. Identify books that will help you become more valuable.

2. Commit to read at least one a month.

3. Commit to read the Bible through in one year.

Chapter Four

THE MOVIES YOU WATCH

> Turn away my eyes from looking at worthless things;
> preserve my life according to your word.
> —Psalm 119:37 (NIV)

There was a great man named Job. This is what Job said and it is good for us all to emulate: "I made a covenant with my eyes" (Job 31:1 NIV). Job knew the power of taking a look and then a double take. Job made up his mind that he would take responsibility for whatever his eyes look at, and for how long. What about you, dear friend? What kinds of movies do you enjoy watching? Movies that are action-packed with a lot of violence?

Some people sit in front of the television set for hours, going from one channel to the other, from one movie to another. They never stop to ask themselves what benefit and relevance these movies and shows are to their individual lives and dreams. No doubt some movies are good and teach some useful lessons about life, but the number of liability movies far outweighs the asset movies. The truth is the eyes are never satisfied with looking, because that is the way they are made to function. The onus is on the individual to control the direction of the eyes. It is doable, but it takes discipline.

In these days of the World Wide Web, people post all sorts of videos on YouTube. If you are not careful, you can get caught up with so many vices and immorality, which lead to pollution. Be mindful of what you watch! You need to break the habit of watching television twenty-four hours a day, seven days a week. It is suicidal!

> In the absence of clearly-defined goals, we become strangely loyal to performing daily trivia until ultimately we become enslaved by it.
> —Robert Heinlein

If you want to be celebrated in your generation, then you must be mindful of the things you do, especially what you feed your eyes with. Of what benefit is it to you to watch every television show? Do not get me wrong, it is good to get entertained but not at the expense of your goals. There is need to exercise restraint so as not to end up wasting enormous amounts of time in the name of entertainment. This only takes one on a road to nowhere.

Action

1. Commit to reducing your time watching movies and TV shows.

2. Choose an area you want to develop in and commit to use your time to educate yourself.

> My interest is in the future because I am going to spend the rest of my life there.
> —Charles Kettering

Chapter Five
WHAT DO YOU DO WITH MONEY?

What you do with money also determines whether you are an asset or a liability. Do you spend your money on liabilities or assets? Wealthy people do not spend heavily on items that will not bring money in return. An average person who has little or no knowledge of how money works (this can be learnt, just like any other skill) will invest in things that do not bring money in return. There are things you can do with money that will not bring more money to you and equally, there are other things you can put money into that will bring a return on your investment. As a young person, you need to know how money works. Invest your time to know more in this area and get started on a life of adventure.

Some years ago, a very young friend of mine who was one of my mentees had imbibed the principle of saving, even as an undergraduate student. He went further to invest in a small-scale business to earn him more money. He became a newspaper agent because he would collect daily newspapers from the publishing house at discounted rates, and the difference between the cost to him and the retail price was his profit. He made money while some of his peers lamented how hard things were. He confided in me that he intended to be his own manager after graduating from college. In other words, he imagined himself as an entrepreneur and an employer of labour. He was not prepared to join the unemployment statistics! He was rare among his peers.

It is amazing how much money you can make with wise spending, either by applying yourself into thinking out of the box or by exchanging some of your leisure time with getting a part-time job. I have discovered that innate in everyone is the entrepreneur that needs to be woken up. You may be sitting on a gold mine as it is now, but if you exercise your thoughts in that direction, money may never come your way. Start small, but dream big!

My advice to the reader of this book, especially the youth, is to acquire knowledge about money and how it works. Do not simply spend money as it comes. I recommend the book *Rich Dad, Poor Dad* by Robert Kiyosaki and Sharon Lechter.

The Bible says, "Wisdom is a shelter as money is a shelter, but the advantage of knowledge is this: Wisdom preserves those who have it" (Eccles. 7:12 NIV). The truth is that once you are able to discipline yourself to read, there are books that will change your paradigm about money. You need wisdom about how money works.

Another book I strongly recommend is *Think and Grow Rich* by Napoleon Hill. The two books I've named are quite small in terms of volume, but they are monumental in impact. Please remember that money does not grow on trees. You must work for it! Riches and wealth locate those who strongly desire it and know that ill-gotten wealth never really lasts. As a matter of fact, money has wings: it can fly to and from you at any time, and that is the reason why you need to first learn how to make money and then make it grow.

Below are five tips on how to manage money.

1. Balance a chequebook
   Start by opening a checking account. Use a register, and learn to use your bank statements to reconcile your account.

2. Budget your money
   Learn how to budget your money. Set up a spending goal. Create a weekly and monthly spending budget. Set up a budget for expenses.

3. Identify wants versus needs
   Use your money to meet only needs, not your wants. There is a difference, and you should know that.

4. Save for the future
   Acquire knowledge about how compound interest works. Learn about the principles of saving a percentage of your income every time you earn money.

5. Stretch a dollar
   Learn the value of a dollar. Set priorities and manage your money. Check out www.kablinga.com to learn how to value money in a fun way.

Those who are assets in their generations have an understanding that money is a servant and not a god to be worshipped. They also understand that like many other talents, you have to learn to master money.

Become an asset!

Action

1. Think about how you can make money.

2. Operate a savings account, and set an amount as a goal.

3. Commit to learn how money works.

Chapter Six
SOME LIABILITIES FEEDERS TO AVOID

There are numerous character traits that feed a person's tendency to become a liability in life. I am going to briefly address some of them below in the hope that if you find that any of these relate to you, you will take action to eliminate them so that you can be an asset. Remember—there is nothing new under the sun. You should face your confrontations; never be ashamed to admit these negative traits. What you don't confront grows! Seek help from people who you know will not condemn you, but will be firm and frank with you to take you to where you want to be. You belong to the top!

Procrastination

> You are the way you are because that's the way you want to be. If you really wanted to be any different, you would be in the process of changing right now.
> —Fred Smith

Procrastination is the act of putting off something requiring immediate attention. Everyone has practiced this at one point in life. Although one may get away with its effect sometimes, it can be very costly. If there is something very important to your future that you must address today, it will pay to focus on it today so that you don't regret it later.

> When you do the things you need to do when you need to do them, the day will come when you can do the things you want to do when you want to do them.
> —Zig Ziglar

Some students put off doing their assignments until it's the last minute, and they cannot produce a quality work, resulting in losing marks they could otherwise have cheaply attained. Some even miss the deadline entirely and get no mark at all. Procrastination steals from you and makes you become a liability. As a matter of fact, people do not like to associate with procrastinators. If you are in the same study group with a procrastinator, he may draw the whole group back and is the weakest link in that group. It is often said that you are as strong as the weakest link. You will miss out on opportunities if you put off what you need to do till later. If you are a procrastinator, you keep pushing the boundaries until it boomerangs in your face.

Procrastination is costly and deadly. When you procrastinate, you can never be an asset to yourself or to your community, unless you break the habit. It is a bad habit, and like every type of habit, it can be learnt and unlearnt. You break the habit by setting goals for yourself.

Set daily SMART goals, and see them through. SMART is an acronym for specific, measurable, achievable, realistic and timely. Every young person wants to be seen as smart. You are truly smart when you can meet your goals in a timely manner. You earn respect by sticking to goals no matter how small. You make little progress consistently until you overcome your weaknesses. It is at this point that you become an asset.

Indecisiveness

> If you want to conquer fear, don't sit at home and think about it. Go out and get busy.
> —Dale Carnegie

Indecision usually works hand in hand with procrastination. If you are indecisive, then you are unable to chart a course to take on any issue. You are unable to commit to something if you are indecisive, and this could make you lose time and opportunities, as well as being very costly. When you are faced with an issue, focus on it, weigh your options quickly and commit. Even if you fail, at least you know that it is not one of the ways to get to what you desire. Indecision breaks focus, and when you lack focus, you cannot be at your best. Indecisiveness is synonymous to being double-minded. Double-mindedness cripples the best of persons. Indecisiveness and self-doubt make one a liability. How would you know what you can achieve if you never have the courage to try? All it takes is to take one tiny step at a time. Be bold, be courageous and make that move right now!

Be an asset!

> All that is necessary to break the spell of inertia and frustration is this: Act as if it were impossible to fail.
> —Dorothea Brande

Fear

> The only thing we have to fear is fear itself.
> —Franklin D. Roosevelt

Fear has been defined as "false evidence appearing real." What are you afraid of? Fear eliminates confidence and faith. You need confidence and faith in order to be an asset in life. Fear says you can't, but faith says you are able! Which will you choose, fear or faith?

> Only when we are no longer afraid do we begin to live.
> —Dorothy Thompson

Dare to believe in yourself. You will never really know whether you can if you don't even try because of fear.

> Do not fear going forward slowly; fear only to stand still.
> —Chinese proverb

Fear paralyses you. Everyone who has become successful overcame fear. Fear is an inner voice that must be silenced! You silence fear by speaking out loud. Say to yourself, "Yes, I can do it!" Truly, you can. You are able to do whatever you set your mind to do. I have come to realize that most people around you may tell you it is impossible, but if you can convince yourself that you are able to do a thing, that is all that matters. If at the end of the day, things do not work out as you envisioned it to be, at least you have tried—and surely you are better off than if you did not try at all.

Face your fears headlong, and it will give way. Dear friend, it is time to confront whatever has been scaring you. What are you waiting for? Go on—take the bull by the horns and tell your success story.

> Our greatest enemies, the ones we must fight most often, are within.
> —Thomas Paine

Low Self-Esteem

> No one can make you feel inferior without your consent.
> —Eleanor Roosevelt

Low self-esteem is one of the major issues that youths face. Every individual is peculiar and unique. There is no one like you in the world. You are special! No one else is like you, and that should make you feel great. You do not have to be like any other person in order to be an asset. You do not have to change your looks to be like someone else. You are you, period, and that is marvellous!

You alone can do what you are purposed to accomplish on earth. That is mind-blowing! Accept yourself, love yourself and get round to doing what you were created for.

People like to put down others for whatever reason. We all fall in that trap. It is up to the recipient to take it as a challenge or buy into that crap. Dear friend, never allow people around you to dictate how you perceive yourself. If you must fight for anything in life, I challenge you to fight against the feeling of being inferior to anyone. You matter! You are on a mission that you alone are able to accomplish. If you mind the naysayers, then you are out of course, and you are a liability because someone needs you—and it could be a matter of life and death!

This book is definitely one of my purposes on earth. Imagine if I didn't write this book. It would never reach your hand, and because you have read this far, I know you are better than when you started reading it, whether consciously or unconsciously. I know somebody somewhere needs to read this book, and if it is just you, then I have achieved my purpose. I believe you get the point. You don't have to affect the whole world; if you can change your mindset about yourself and make that shift, which will affect even a handful of people, then you are a success and an asset! Don't leave a vacuum. Achieve and be an asset!

> If you just set out to be liked, you would be prepared to compromise on anything at anytime, and you would achieve nothing.
> —Margaret Thatcher

Ignorance

Ignorance is not having the right knowledge for a given issue. Ignorance is very costly and makes you vulnerable to being exploited and deceived. There are many downsides to ignorance. The cure for ignorance is knowledge. That is why you must constantly seek to know! On matters that concern your future, your life and your very being, you must be knowledgeable. Exert yourself to acquire knowledge; you will be surprised how much you do not know. There are some vital life tools that are not taught at school, and you have to discover them yourself. It pays to know!

When you are knowledgeable, you cannot be easily cheated. For example, know your rights as a person, the law concerning any given subject matter of interest and your strengths so you can gear them towards your goals in life. Know what you are capable of doing, the people you associate with and what they are about. Do not grope in the dark.

Knowledge truly is power. Once you know, there is a floodgate of light, and darkness is destroyed for good. What you learn, no one can take from you. You acquire knowledge in very many ways, but first there has to be a desire to know. Once you desire to know, you will inevitably encounter people who are knowledgeable in that field of interest. Then it is up to you to approach them or read their books, their blogs, the Internet or whatever means available to acquire the knowledge. Sometimes it will cost you money, and it will always cost you devoting the time to learn. Be ready to spend the time to acquire knowledge. Knowledge makes you an asset. Be an asset!

Examples of Liabilities

Satan

Satan is the greatest liability to the human race. He was a liability to Adam and Eve, and he is still a liability to people who allow him. He is described in the Bible as "The thief comes only to steal and kill and destroy" (John 10:10a NIV). He comes in subtle ways to rob us of diverse things, including our very existence and purpose. It is only those who have given their lives wholly to Jesus who are truly born again and are living spirit-filled lives who have the power to avoid falling into his traps. Beware and watch out! Satan is our number-one liability. He subtly crept into Adam's and Eve's lives, and he is still doing the same today, especially in the lives of the youth. He comes and says, "Just try it. It won't harm you just this once ..." He uses the voice of your friends or peers, and you fall for it because you want to belong to the crowd. He comes to some young girls with words of deceit: "Go for a night out with some good-looking guy." Inevitably the girls lose the most precious thing in their lives: their innocence. One thing leads to the other—pregnancy, abortion, murder, venereal diseases, HIV and AIDS and untimely death.

Satan is still using those dirty old tricks. The apple is full of worms, so beware! Like Joseph, I advise you to cut away and run for your life. Why must your destiny be cut short? Joseph was a young man who found himself far away from home and his loved ones, yet he decided to guard his morals. Many young people in Joseph's shoes would throw caution to the winds and say, "It doesn't matter." Of course it matters. Joseph was enticed by his master's wife. The coast was clear, and Joseph could easily have given in, but he could smell the worms in the apple from afar; he knew this was Satan's wicked strategy to cut short his destiny. Guess what Joseph did? He took to his heels and ran as fast as he could to get away from that situation. If he had waited for a second, he would have been trapped, and the story would have been different. What Joseph did is exactly what every young person should do. You should vigorously guard your destiny. It is far better to remain unsullied than to destroy your destiny in the face of instant gratification.

> Learn to see in another's calamity the ills that you should avoid.
> —Thomas Jefferson

Samson and Delilah

The story in the book of Judges about a man named Samson is still very relevant for today's youth. Samson was born to fulfill a great destiny, and his parents were specifically instructed about how their child should be raised. Samson was well informed about how he was a special individual. In Judges 16, at a point during his youth, he went to a place called the Valley of Sorek and met a woman called Delilah. He fell in love with Delilah. Unknown to Samson, this same Delilah had made a pact with Samson's enemies, who were determined to destroy him. Delilah succeeded in her mission—and made some money too. As for Samson, that was the end of his great life. He went to the valley and was not able to rise up anymore.

Delilah was a huge liability in Samson's life, yet Samson did not know it until he was captured by his enemies. Delilah was working for his enemies, yet Samson was most comfortable around her. She was a friendly enemy! She was a distraction for Samson that eventually cost him his life. Delilah was able to succeed in breaking the source of Samson's strength. Some people around us break our concentration and cause us to lose focus. If you identify such people, it is best to avoid them like a plague.

Samson, like every single one of us, was a destiny child with a unique purpose, and he knew it. You will know whether there is something unique about you. As a matter of fact, Samson was told specifically what to avoid in order to stay in his purpose. The whole world knew about this strange young man, and some set of people, particularly the Philistines, were scared about his exploits and were ready to do all they could to end Samson's life. Yet Samson chose to take a girlfriend from among his enemies. Delilah was attracted to Samson, but she was more committed to her people and was determined to rob Samson of his power. Samson was also physically attracted to Delilah and chose to ignore the spiritual implication for him. He probably thought it did not matter and underestimated his enemies, the Philistines (Delilah's kinsmen). The result was tragic and led to the end of a monumental destiny!

It will be a tragedy if you are robbed of all you are destined to be, simply because you are unable to hold yourself back from instant gratification. There are lots of ways you can cut yourself short. If you indulge in premarital sex, pornography, masturbation, fornication, serial dating, drugs, alcohol or clubbing, you are setting yourself up for a great fall just like Samson.

A note of warning to the youth: Be careful whom you fall in love with, because he or she may be the devil's agent sent specifically to destroy your destiny. By the way, if you are in a relationship, and your partner tells you to keep it a secret so no one knows about it, you are treading a dangerous path. Do not fall in love blindly—open your eyes and seek counsel. Do not take your heart on a journey without your head. Some people say love is blind. That is an erroneous thought. I often advise young, unmarried people to endeavour to know who they intend to marry, but this is a subject for another day.

> We must all suffer from one of two pains: the pain of discipline or the pain of regret. The difference is discipline weighs ounces while regret weighs tons.
> —Jim Rohn

King Solomon and His Concubines

Solomon was the wisest man who ever lived, and at the end of his life, he confessed, "'Meaningless! Meaningless!' says the Teacher. 'Everything is meaningless!'" (Eccles. 12:8 NIV). Solomon had 700 wives and 300 concubines. All these women drew his heart away from the source of his wisdom, and his kingdom was eventually torn apart. With whom do you surround yourself? Who are your friends and advisors? Watch out for liabilities! It is possible to be derailed from your destiny by your association. This has been proven to be true many times over. It is better to have one quality friend than to have a vast array of acquaintances who add no value to your existence. You have the choice!

> Choice, not chance, determines human destiny.
> —Robert W. Ellis

Action

1. Commit to eliminating liabilities in your life.

2. Seek ways to insulate yourself from negative traits.

Chapter Seven
ASSET BUILDING BLOCKS

The whole essence of this book lies in this chapter. It will be to your benefit to pay attention to some of the pertinent attributes outlined below. To me, these attributes will inevitably catapult you to being the best you can be.

Planning

> Create a definite plan for carrying out your desire and begin at once, whether you are ready or not, to put this plan into action.
> —Napoleon Hill

Planning is a major building block to becoming an asset. As I said earlier, to fail to prepare is to prepare to fail, and that is true with regards to all aspects of life, whether it's school, your future career, seeking opportunities, getting married, retirement, sports—you name it. Everything answers to planning. Planning is the key!

Journaling is an excellent way to start planning. A majority of the time, what you have written down does get at least a 70 percent chance of getting done. That has been my personal experience, and it has worked for me. I write down things I want to do and achieve in the short term and long term. The next step is to break down the plan into small bits and tackle them one at a time. By doing so, you make progress and eventually succeed as you stick to the plan.

> A clear vision, backed by definite plans, gives you a tremendous feeling of confidence and personal power.
> —Brian Tracy

Discipline

> Like a city whose walls are broken through is a person who lacks self-control.
> —Proverbs 25:28 (NIV)

Discipline is the key. Discipline is being under control or rules. It builds a strong character, which is a necessary ingredient to success and becoming an asset. Discipline goes hand in hand with integrity and involves your ability to say no to something that you know will cause you to derail from your goals, and to say yes to others that will enhance your success. Most of the time, it is a call for painful denial of a temporary enjoyment or the undertaking of a difficult task that you would rather not do, but for the fact that you want to succeed. Discipline is an inevitable piece of becoming an asset. The fact that everybody is embarking on a certain direction is irrelevant. The question for you is, "Will this venture add or take from me?" You make the judgment call!

> No discipline seems pleasant at the time, but painful. Later on, however, it produces a harvest of righteousness and peace for those who have been trained by it.
> —Hebrews 12:11 (NIV)

Discipline differentiates the person who is an asset from the person who is a liability. That is why some folks have classmates who have gone on to achieve great things and are still achieving, whereas others are still wondering, "What on earth is happening to me?" Discipline is the X factor! Everyone has something to offer, but not everyone has the inbuilt discipline to deliver to the waiting world. If it has to be, it's up to you. It is your choice. Be an asset, not a liability!

Self-Confidence

> So do not throw away your confidence; it will be richly rewarded.
> —Hebrews 10:35 (NIV)

Self-confidence is about believing in your brand—you! Yes, you are your own brand. You should believe in your abilities and walk tall no matter the external pressure you experience.

> People die of fright and live of confidence.
> —Henry David Thoreau

Self-confidence comes from within. The truth is if you do not believe in yourself, you can never become an asset. Here are some steps you can take to increase your self-confidence.

1. Learn to challenge the inner voice that says, "I can't." If you practice this long enough, you will conquer self-doubt.

    > I can do all this through him who gives me strength.
    > —Philippians 4:13 (NIV)

2. Identify your strengths and then develop those strengths to make them even better.

3. Acknowledge your weaknesses and then acquire knowledge about how to overcome them.

    > The wise prevail through great power, and those who have knowledge muster their strength.
    > —Proverbs 24:5 (NIV)

4. Never dwell on your weaknesses. People around you may enlarge your weaknesses, but no one is perfect. Thank them for pointing out the areas where you have room to grow, but never let their criticism stop you from being an asset.

   The discerning heart seeks knowledge, but the
   mouth of a fool feeds on folly.
   —Proverbs 15:14 (NIV)

5. Use your talent to help others. Your gifts may offer a solution to someone else's problem, so focus on that!

   Do not neglect the gift.
   —1 Timothy 4:14a (NIV)

   For this reason I remind you to fan into flame the
   gift of God, which is in you …
   —2 Timothy 1:6 (NIV)

   A gift makes opens the way and ushers the giver into
   the presence of the great.
   —Proverbs 18:16 (NIV)

As you focus on your talent and endeavour to use it to help others, there is a guarantee that your talent will announce you to your world. You never know where that little step will take you. The world is your horizon. Be an asset!

> You need to overcome the tug of people against you
> as you reach for high goals.
> —General George Patton

Mentors and Role Models

> Plans are established by seeking advice.
> —Proverbs 20:18 (NIV)

I have come to understand that you can learn from other people's experiences and avoid unnecessary mistakes. There is nothing new under the sun. What you are experiencing now, someone, somewhere, sometime has also gone through it. You can learn from them and save yourself undue stress, time and energy.

> For lack of guidance a nation falls, but victory is won through many advisers.
> —Proverbs 11:14 (NIV)

You can also ask someone who has been down the path you want to take to become your mentor. Successful people are generally willing to share their experiences with others. Consulting the learned is a win-win situation. Read, listen to and observe role models. Take that risk and reach out in trust to get advice.

> Plans fail for lack of counsel, but with many advisers they succeed.
> —Proverbs 15:22 (NIV)

It may cost you to search out a mentor that really suits your vision, but give it that energy because it will pay off. It may even cost you some money, but the value you get will far outweigh the cost. Remember—it is all about you! You have to fulfill your own call—no one will do it for you.

Give it all it takes. Be an asset!

Persistence

> Failure should be our teacher, not our undertaker. Failure is delay not defeat. It is a temporary detour, not a dead end.
> —Denis Waitley

Persistence is staying power in the face of failure. It is a vital block in building a life and being an asset. Everything in life needs a push in order to achieve a goal, and most times you need to be pushed again and again. That is where persistence comes in.

> When nothing seems to help, I go and look at a stonecutter hammering away at his rock perhaps a hundred times without as much as a crack showing in it. Yet at the hundred and first blow it will split in two, and I know it was not that blow that did it—but all that had gone before.
> —Jacob Riis

The above quote translates to the fact that you should never give up easily. It also speaks to determination knowing that it is achievable. You can be whatever you want to be, go wherever you want to go, and achieve any goal by using persistence and other building blocks.

> Perseverance is failing 19 times and succeeding the 20th.
> —Julie Andrews

In Luke 11:5–8 (NIV), there is an analogy about persistence.

> And He said to them, "which of you shall have a friend, and go to him at midnight and say to him, 'Friend, lend me three loaves;

> For a friend of mine has come to me on his journey, and I have nothing to set before him';
>
> And he will answer from within and say, 'Do not trouble me; the door is now shut, and my children are with me in bed; I cannot rise and give to you'?
>
> I say to you, though he will not rise and give to him because he is his friend, yet because of his *persistence* he will rise and give him as many as he needs. (emphasis mine)

In that story, a person has gone to his friend at midnight to ask for a favour. Usually you would ask during the day, but for some reason this fellow needed the help in the midnight hour, where it is almost impossible to get the needed attention from his friend. As a matter of fact, his friend told him off and asked him to scram, but this guy persisted. He was desperate and would not take no for an answer. Guess what? He got what he wanted because of his persistence!

If you are persistent, doors that others say cannot be opened will open for you! Never give up! PUSH stands for "push until something happens."

> The future has several names. For the weak, it is the impossible. For the fainthearted, it is the unknown. For the thoughtful and valiant, it is the ideal.
> —Victor Hugo

Determination

> The only difference between successful people and unsuccessful people is extraordinary determination.
> —Mary Kay Ash

When faced with an obstacle, it is determination that makes you stay and face that challenge, instead of running away. It is only a challenge, and you must not quit. Quitters never win! Challenges in any area of life test how much inner power you have developed. If you stay long enough, the challenge will be surmounted, and you will be better for it. Give it all it takes. Be determined to succeed. Be determined to be an asset.

> I am willing to put myself through anything; temporary pain or discomfort means nothing to me as long as I can see that the experience will take me to a new level.
> —Diana Nyad

There is an interesting story about determination in the book of Ruth. In Ruth, chapter 1, we read of a woman, Naomi, who had lost her husband and two sons in a foreign country. To Naomi, all was lost, and she decided to return to her homeland because she has nothing to offer her two daughters-in-law. One of the daughters-in-law decided to seek another life without Naomi, and rightly so. But Ruth was determined to follow Naomi wherever Naomi went. It turned out that her determination paid off for Ruth at the end, because she married a rich man from Naomi's kindred eventually and became celebrated for her determination.

Ruth could not be deterred. In Ruth 1:18, even Naomi could not stop Ruth from following her. Everything looked bad and gloomy. Ruth could taste failure, but she refused to be deterred. Naomi could not stop her from following her to an unknown destiny. "When Naomi realized that Ruth was determined to go with her, she stopped urging her" (Ruth 1:18 NIV).

Dear friend, never take no for an answer. If you desire something, go for it! You must surely be celebrated!

Examples of Assets

David and Jonathan

There is a profound story about two friends in the Bible, David and Jonathan. David happened to have been employed by Jonathan's father, King Saul. David and Jonathan became very good friends, to the point that when Saul plotted to kill David, Jonathan told David of his father's evil plan and facilitated David's escape.

They were good friends even in death, and after death. Jonathan saved David's life in the face of being robbed of his throne as heir apparent. David remained faithful to Jonathan even after he had died and showed favour to his crippled son.

Such friendships are rare today but still exist. You come by such relationships as you make yourself a friendly person and pray for good friends. As parents, we must pray that our children will meet with godly friends who will be assets to their destinies. Every parent should fervently pray for this.

Friends who are assets have the characteristics that Jonathan had. They will always protect you from danger and hazards. They will not encourage you to indulge in premarital sex, prostitution, occultism or drugs. They will assist you in achieving your dreams. They will not be envious and will not seek ways to derail you from your laudable goals. These types of friends will give good advice, even to their own disadvantage.

My friend, I encourage you today to check again. What character traits do you see in that so-called best friend? If you see negative traits, it is time to make another best friend. It is your choice!

Joshua and Caleb

Life is full of obstacles, and only the brave and bold can keep going in the face of these challenges. There is a saying that nothing moves unless a greater force is applied. In every facet of life, some form of exertion is required to make even the smallest headway. This is why the story of Joshua and Caleb in the Bible is so intriguing.

The Israelites had left Egypt after being in bondage for about 400 years. They had crossed the Red Sea on dry ground and had been in the wilderness for another 40 years. They had reached a land called the promised land, and 12 young men were sent by their leader to scout the land and come up with a strategy to possess it. Ten of the young spies saw giants and came up with a terrifying report, but two saw things differently. Joshua and Caleb came with a favourable report of hope and optimism—what we call today the can-do spirit. The majority saw obstacles and barriers, but the minority saw opportunity!

Joshua and Caleb spied the land of Canaan, and they encouraged and convinced each other that they could capture the land. They were positive even though others saw things differently. Who encourages you to go on in life? Who is rooting for you as you play the game of life? That person is an asset to you. Joshua and Caleb had the can-do spirit and believed that God could not fail and that it was a worthwhile exploration.

What kind of attitude do you have when faced with challenges? What do your friends think about challenges? Obstacles are merely a call to strengthen you. Do not weaken your resolve to achieve worthwhile goals. Between you and anything significant, there will be giants in your path!

> If you want to achieve a high goal, you're going to have to take some chances.
> —Alberto Salazar

For that project you intend to embark on, or that course or programme you desire to pursue—what do you see? Do you see impossibilities or possibilities? Those who see possibilities even in the face of obstacles can become nothing but assets.

I encourage you to confront your confrontations!

You can make it! Yes, you will!

> You need to overcome the tug of people against you as you reach for high goals.
> —General George Patton

> When you believe and think "I can," you activate your motivation, commitment, confidence, concentration and excitement—all of which relate directly to achievement.
> —Dr. Jerry Lynch

> You'll always miss 100% of the shots you don't take.
> —Wayne Gretzky

Jesus Christ

May I introduce a friend to you. His name is Jesus Christ. He wants to make you His friend. His arms are wide open. Here is how the Bible describes Him: a friend who sticks closer than a brother!

Jesus Christ is the greatest asset one can ever have. Read this!

> Very rarely will anyone die for a righteous person, though for a good person someone might possibly dare to die. But God demonstrates his own love for us in this: While we were still sinners, Christ died

> for us. For if, while we were God's enemies, we were reconciled to him through the death of his Son, how much more, having been reconciled, shall we be saved through his life!
> —Romans 5:7–8, 10 (NIV)

The Holy Spirit

The Holy Spirit is an invaluable asset. He is our comforter, guide, helper, strength, standby and powerhouse! "But when he, the Spirit of truth, comes, he will guide you into all the truth. He will not speak on his own; he will speak only what he hears, and he will tell you what is yet to come" (John 16:13 NIV).

The Holy Spirit is also a teacher. He teaches truth and wisdom. He teaches about all things, and that includes both what they teach and what they do not teach at school. He tells you what you ordinarily may not know and what you need to succeed.

We all need a friend like the gentle Holy Spirit! In order for Him to become your friend, you have to accept and believe in Jesus Christ. That is the only way the Holy Spirit can befriend you. I can assure you that whatever the Holy Spirit teaches you is the truth.

> You do not succeed because you do not know what you want or you don't want it intensely enough.
> —Frank Crane

> A vision is a clearly-articulated, results-oriented picture of a future you intend to create. It is a dream with direction.
> —Jesse Stoner Zemel

Action

1. Commit to creating time to do a personal retreat and a self-examination.

2. Ask for the help of the Holy Spirit to be a person of value.

3. Take steps to be an asset and make a difference.

Chapter Eight
A DESTINY TO FULFILL

Life is a journey. You need to ask yourself honest questions as you lay the foundation for your journey in life. Ask yourself, "What is my destination? What do I want to attain? Do I want to be fulfilled and secure?" Your answer is very important because it will determine how you position yourself and which route you take. Foundations are vital to your building! "When the foundations are being destroyed, what can the righteous do?" (Ps. 11:3 NIV). You must lay the right foundation so that you can build confidently.

What is your goal? A goal is different from a wish. If you do not translate a wish to a goal by taking practical steps, then you will remain a wishful thinker. You must have a vision as to what, where, who and how you want to eventually turn out to be. For some people, anything goes; for others, they say time will tell. The wise person first thinks through it before starting out. Why? So that when obstacles, delays and trials come, they are able to overcome them.

> Vision without action is a daydream. Action without vision is a nightmare.
> —Japanese proverb

What do you value most? Determining what you value most now will save you many agonising decisions and sleepless nights later. You are not a mistake on planet earth—you are here for a purpose!

What is that purpose? What mark do you want to leave on the sands of time?

While growing up, I learnt a poem titled "Solomon Grundy," which is about a man who was known simply because he only occupied space on planet earth but never added any value in any shape or form. "Solomon Grundy" was someone with no visions, goals or any form of motivation. Do you want to become a Solomon Grundy? I assume not. Therefore, you must rise up!

Write down your goals and the plans you want to achieve. Then, as opportunities come your way, grab them with both hands and fulfill your destiny. It is a matter of choice, and the world needs you! You are an answer to someone's questions. You are the ray of light to someone's darkness.

> Until you commit your goals to paper, you have intentions that are seeds without soil.
> —anonymous

Too many people wander through life without a plan, and all the while, their most precious asset, time, is fleeting by. This does not have to happen to you. On this note, I leave you with this.

> Make your mark. You can choose to be a settler or a pioneer. Settlers just settle. They mark themselves "present" in life's attendance register but are "absent" in life's achievement register. Pioneers make a difference. They are barrier breakers. They go where no one has gone. They achieve the impossible. The spirit of a pioneer rests upon you. You've got the power. Go Ahead! Dazzle the world with your brilliance!
> —Mensa Otabil

Be an asset, not a liability!

> It's not where you start—it's where you finish that counts.
> —Zig Ziglar

Chapter Nine
CONFESSIONS FOR SUCCESS

If you want to see yourself transform into what you desire to become, you have to change your language. What you say about yourself determines to a large extent what you actually become. It starts with your thought pattern and then affects your words, and it keeps going in a cycle. You say, then you think and then you become!

In this chapter, I have listed some power language. It is up to you to create the future for yourself. Tell yourself the statements below many times in a day, and if possible, stand in front of the mirror. Most adolescents spend a considerable amount of time in front of the mirror anyway, so you might as well use the time constructively! Begin to speak out loud these statements.

I am great!
I am unique!
I am original!
I am an asset!
I am in charge!
I am a finisher!
I am free to become!
I will fulfill my destiny!
I am the pilot of my time!
I can be the best I can be!
I am a winner, not a loser!
I am an asset, not a liability!
I am a success, not a failure!

I can accomplish great things!
I am an overcomer, not a victim!
I am a high flyer and an achiever!
I have faith and hope in my future!
I have a colourful and bright future!
Everything is working for my good!
I will stand out and become outstanding!
Every day, in every way, I am changing for the better!

Successful people form the habit of doing what failures don't like to do. They like the results they get by doing what they don't necessarily enjoy.
—Earl Nightingale

Action

1. Say the confession three times daily.

2. Believe in yourself and exhibit self-confidence.

Chapter Ten

DANIEL—A CASE STUDY

There is a story of a youth who was not only an asset in his lifetime, but even thousands of years after he had died, he is still a model for youths in any generation. His name is Daniel, and you can find his story in the Bible, in the book named after him. I recommend that every youth reads his story over and over. A closer look into his life will give us insight as to how to be an asset in life. Come along with me as I highlight some qualities in his life.

Daniel's Background

He was a Jew by birth from a royal and noble family, and it is recorded that he was handsome and had an aptitude for learning. He was well informed and quick to understand; however, he had challenges because he was captured as a slave for Babylon.

Daniel as a Slave

He was selected along with other young Jewish boys to serve the ruling king, and he had to undergo three years' training in the language and literature of the Babylonians. However, he resolved that he would remain true to himself—he insisted that he not defile himself! He decided to take charge of what he ate and drank, and more important, he carefully selected who his close associates were. He surrounded himself with people of like mind, and impeccable character. They feared God and encouraged one another.

Daniel's Abilities

Daniel had the ability to understand visions and dreams of all kinds. He recognized this about himself and developed and used it to the fullest for his advantage. He was unequalled and outstanding in his generation. He was known to have been 10 times better than his contemporaries. He spoke with wisdom and tact and was sensitive to timing.

Daniel was a person of integrity, trustworthy and hardworking, and he was self-confident. He was a problem solver and had solutions to problems around him. He was able to distinguish himself with this exceptional quality, and he was an asset to three kings.

Daniel honoured God by putting Him first. He had the Spirit of God in him, and he actively ensured his relationship with God was maintained. He read the scriptures daily, prayed about three times a day, fasted and was quick to repent for himself and on behalf of others. He wrote down every of his visions and dreams that were revealed to him, and he prophesied about events that would occur thousands of years in the future.

Daniel was unique and unstoppable. I encourage you to take time to read about this youth in the Bible. Just like Daniel, every youth can be an asset!

Daniel had every reason to deny his faith, become bitter, associate with folks who could have been bad influences on his life, be disillusioned and never hope for a brighter future. But he determined to not let his present circumstances truncate his visions and dreams. He placed a high value on his relationship with God and trusted God to make something excellent out of his hopeless circumstances. Sure enough, he triumphed. You too can pick up courage now no matter your present circumstances or failures. It is not too late, and it's certainly not over until it is over! Get up! Go back to school or college, get educated, be the best you can be in your chosen vocation and add value to the world around you. Never give up on yourself. You are much more valuable than you think. The world needs you. You can rewrite your story, even now.

Read this chapter again and see what areas you can emulate from the life of Daniel. Take time to work on these areas—you'll be better for it.

Action

1. Think of one skill you are good at.

2. Commit to spending time to improve that skill.

Chapter Eleven

THE RIGHT TO CHOOSE

Life is full of choices. You choose to succeed or fail. You choose whether or not to wear that dress or shirt today. You choose to do one thing or the other. There is also a great choice to make. Choose Jesus Christ if you want to be an asset in your generation. This is His promise to you in John 10:10, which says, "I have come that they may have life, and have it to the full." What a promise, to have a life that is an asset to your generation! Without Jesus, you end up in the hands of the greatest liability of all times, Satan, and you end up living a life full of liabilities: failure, disappointment, rejection, depression, sickness and disease. That is a life full of misery, and who wants that? I don't, and neither do you. There is no middle ground. Choose Jesus Christ for a life of greatest asset!

I accepted Jesus Christ through reading a book. That book was an asset to me, and I want this to be the same to you. Jesus said, "Very truly I tell you, no one can see the kingdom of God unless they are born again" (John 3:3 NIV). What does it take to be born again? You simply believe in your heart and confess with your mouth that Jesus is Lord. You do not need to do anything more than that. It is by faith! It is easy, but it is simply by choice. In Romans 3:23 (NIV), the Bible says, "For all have sinned and fall short of the glory of God," but thank God, Jesus came to restore that glory! We are unable to save ourselves through good works, giving of alms or doing some religious act. Salvation is a relationship, not religion! It is a personal relationship with Jesus Christ. That is what God is offering you through this medium.

I know you want to be an asset. I know, because you have read this far. Now, all you need to do is say this prayer and mean it with all your heart. Say this out loud, "Lord Jesus, I come to You today. I know I am a sinner, and I believe You are my saviour. You died and rose again, and You are Lord. I invite You into my heart and ask that You save me today, for I am a sinner. I receive You into my life. Be my Lord and master. Thank You for saving me. Amen." Congratulations!

Action Steps for a New Beginning

1. Go to a Bible-believing church, where you will learn how to live the successful Christian life, and where your pastor and Christian family can help you and encourage you in your new faith.

2. Get baptised by immersion in water, in obedience to the Word of God.

3. Study your Bible daily. Start with the Gospel of John and other New Testament books. Get a version of the Bible you can easily understand, and ask the Holy Spirit to reveal the Bible's truth and power to you. The precious Holy Spirit is the teacher and comforter who now lives inside of you!

4. Pray always. There's no need to use fancy words. Simply speak to your God. He will answer your prayers and guide you.

5. Live a holy life by living in accordance to the instructions of the Bible.

Chapter Twelve
GO AND SUCCEED

One of the tragedies in life is to live a purposeless life without impact. In this book, I have tried to direct you to some of the ways you can make your life count as a youth. It is never too late to take the right steps, and no one is too young to be an asset. If you put your mind and heart to it and give yourself a chance, you will be able to prove to yourself and the world that the sky is the limit. The ground is too crowded, and there is so much room in the sky for you to spread your wings and fly.

You don't have to be someone else, because you are an original and unique! Everyone has a destiny to fulfill, and that is the essence of this book: to let you know that someone in this world needs you. You are the solution to someone's problem. All may not need you, but if you can make a difference to someone, that is being an asset.

Being successful and being an asset is not determined by material acquisitions, although there is nothing evil about that. It is about making a difference in someone's life, and that can be done in so many ways. You must begin by doing the following:

1. Separate yourself from bad company.

2. Invest your time wisely.

3. Seek knowledge and wisdom.

4. Watch what you feed your mind.

5. Manage your resources, and be prudent.

6. Speak the right words, and exercise faith.

7. Pay attention to those who have gone through the same path before.

8. Learn from the mistakes of others.

9. Hold tightly to divine guidance by the Holy Spirit.

10. Humbly walk with your maker.

No one is on earth by accident or mistake. You are here with a specific purpose that you and you alone can execute. If you fail to do that, then you have only come to be a liability in your generation, and you will be failing humanity as a whole.

Think and ask yourself, "How can I become an asset? What am I wired for?" If you are able to figure that out, then go for it and don't stop until you make it. When you make up your mind to be an asset and not a liability, you can only succeed! Go succeed—be an asset! Stand out in your generation! Be outstanding! Be a high flyer! The world is waiting for you. Be a shining star! Yes, you can, and you will!

See you at the topmost top!

Action

1. Commit to overcoming obstacles and barriers.

2. Recommend this book to someone.

ABOUT THE YOUNG, FREE AND SINGLE FORUM

The Young, Free and Single Forum was started by Olayinka Ekenkwo, who founded Hephzibah Movement Worldwide. The forum focuses on topical issues specifically targeted at youths by way of inspiring, interactive and educational seminars and by utilizing a variety of activities, such as music, drama, talent hunt, talk shows on handling relationships and career choices, debates, networking and candid questions and answers.

The Young, Free and Single Forum was created to impact youths for success and provide the needed support and guidance that are rarely taught in the schools but that are necessary tools to live successful lives.

The passion for youths has increased in Olayinka's heart since her relocation to Canada. She is determined to make a difference in the lives of any young person who will give her the privilege to do so.

Printed in the United States
By Bookmasters